# Introduction

Imagine yourself a scientist who collects insects, spiders, and other creepy, crawly creatures most people call *bugs*. You would want to get a close look at the bugs' parts—bodies, heads, and legs—and how they connect together. The collection of parts in this kit lets you do just that.

Follow the easy, step-by-step instructions on the next four pages to build five different bugs: ladybug, black ant, stag beetle, greenbottle fly, and orb weaver spider. The bugs you can build using this kit will all be about the same size, so you can mix and match parts to create new kinds of bugs. To the right is a comparison of their real sizes.

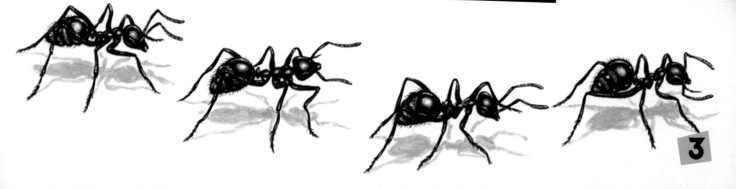

# Assembly Instructions

Build a ladybug, black ant, stag beetle, greenbottle fly, and orb weaver spider. To follow are two illustrations of each bug: an "exploded" view that shows how to fit the parts together, and a picture of what the bug should look like once it's assembled. Try building all five bugs at once, or mix and match the bodies, heads, legs, and wings and make up a new kind of bug!

## Ladybug

The ladybug has a red body and head. Insert the peg on the head into the hole at the front of the body. The legs are numbered on the bottom: 1, 2, 3, 4, 5, and 6. Insert the peg on each leg into the corresponding leg hole.

# Totally

# BUGS

By Dennis Schatz

Illustrations by Peter Georgeson

*To Leila, who helped me appreciate a bug's life.*

**Silver Dolphin Books**
An imprint of the Baker & Taylor Publishing Group
10350 Barnes Canyon Road, San Diego, CA 92121
www.silverdolphinbooks.com

Book text © 2000, 2013 by Dennis Schatz
Cover and interior illustrations © 2000, 2013 by Peter Georgeson
Illustrations on pages 4, 5, 6, and 7 © 2000, 2013 by Sylvia Shapiro
Illustrations on pages 14, 15, 22, and 23 © 2000, 2013 by Bob Greisen
© 2013 becker&mayer! LLC

ISBN-13: 978-1-60710-787-3
ISBN-10: 1-60710-787-2

*Totally Bugs* is produced by becker&mayer!, Bellevue, Washington
www.beckermayer.com

Manufactured, printed, and assembled in He Yuan City, China.

1 2 3 4 5 17 16 15 14 13

12466

Fact card writer: Robin Cruise
Fact card editor: Betsy Henry Pringle
Editor: Jennifer Doyle
Book designers: Two Pollard Design
Cover designer: Scott Westgard
Typesetting by Sheila VanNortwick
Photo researcher: Kara Stokes
Production coordinator: Diane Ross

Photo Credits: Cards and poster: ladybug on flower © irin-k/Shutterstock; black ant
© kingfisher/Shutterstock; orb weaver spider © Bill Kennedy/Shutterstock; stag beetle © Karel Gallas/Shutterstock; dragonfly © Mircea BEZERGHEANU/Shutterstock;
greenbottle fly on flower © Ian Grainger/Shutterstock; monarch butterfly © James
Laurie/Shutterstock; blue morpho butterfly © Brenda Carson/Shutterstock; luna
moth © Cathy Keifer/Shutterstock; praying mantis © Florian Andronache/
Shutterstock; stick insect © Stephane Bidouze/Shutterstock; jewel scarab © Nathan
B Dappen/Shutterstock; leaf-cutter ant © Eric Isselée/Shutterstock; treehopper ©
Suede Chen/Shutterstock; cicada © Roger Meerts/Shutterstock; grasshopper © Sean
van Tonder/Shutterstock; cricket © Wong Hock weng/Shutterstock; honeybee ©
Mircea BEZERGHEANU/Shutterstock; wasp © Kurt_G/Shutterstock; termite © Pan
Xunbin/Shutterstock; cockroach © Dmitrijs Mihejevs/Shutterstock; caterpillar © Igor
Semenov/Shutterstock; firefly © Fer Gregory/Shutterstock; Hercules beetle © Kowit
Sitthi/Shutterstock; stag beetles fighting © sergyiway/Shutterstock.

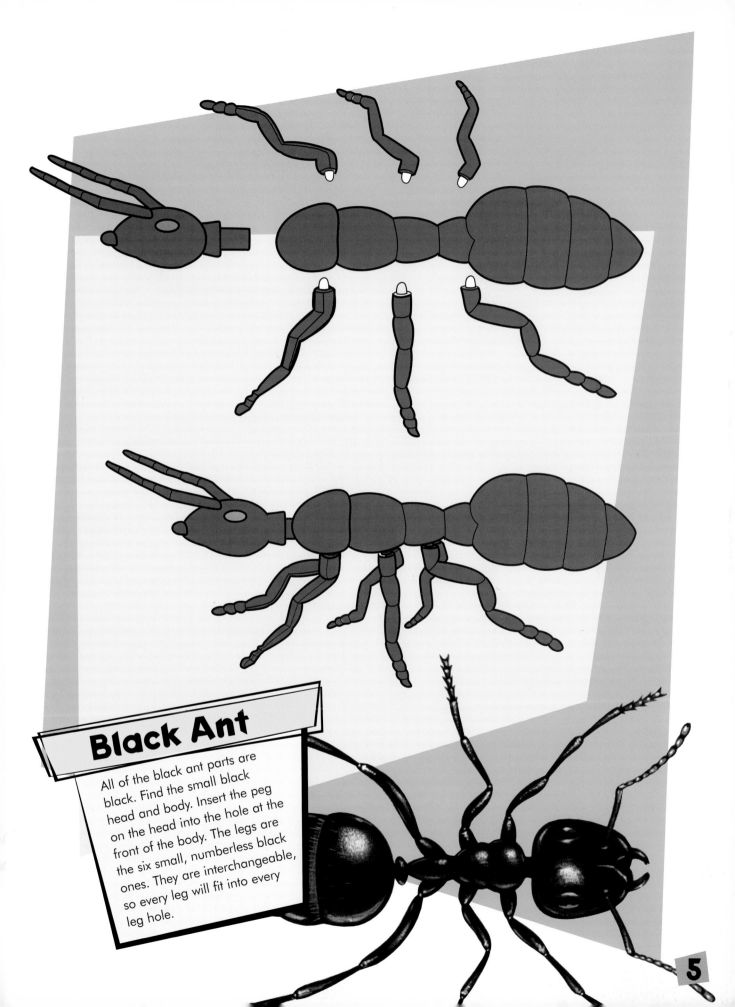

# Black Ant

All of the black ant parts are black. Find the small black head and body. Insert the peg on the head into the hole at the front of the body. The legs are the six small, numberless black ones. They are interchangeable, so every leg will fit into every leg hole.

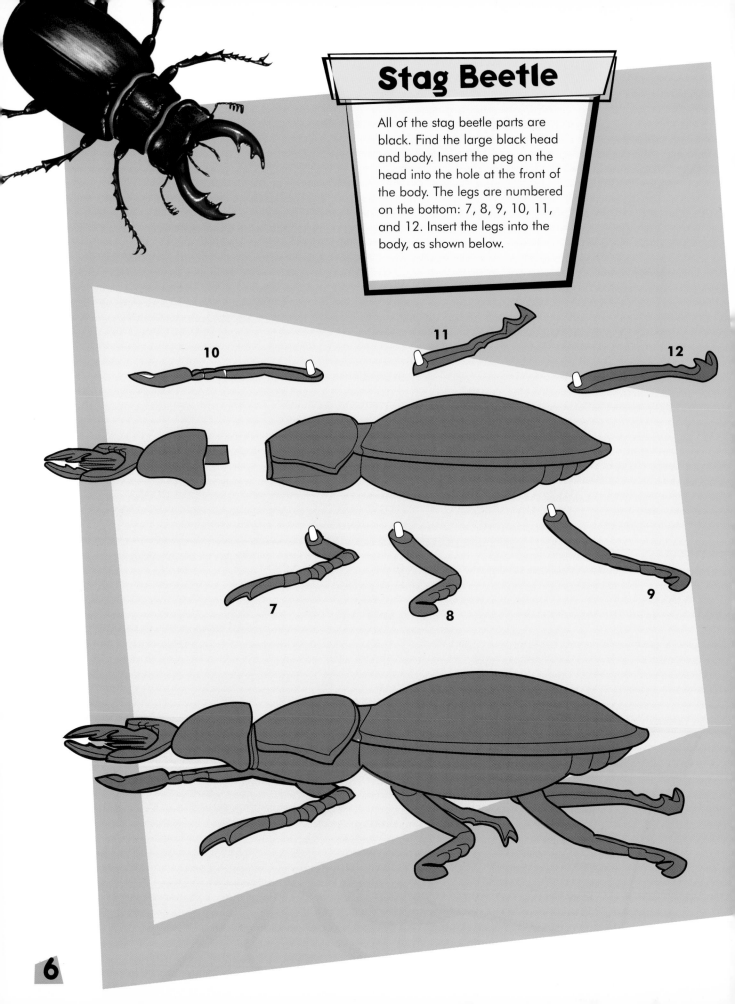

# Stag Beetle

All of the stag beetle parts are black. Find the large black head and body. Insert the peg on the head into the hole at the front of the body. The legs are numbered on the bottom: 7, 8, 9, 10, 11, and 12. Insert the legs into the body, as shown below.

# Greenbottle Fly

All of the greenbottle fly parts are green. Find the green body, head, and legs. Insert the peg on the head into the hole at the front of the body. The legs are interchangeable, so every leg will fit into every leg hole. The fly also has clear wings that plug into its back.

# Orb Weaver Spider

All of the orb weaver spider parts are yellow-brown. Find the yellow-brown body, head, and legs. Insert the peg on the head into the hole at the front of the body. The legs are numbered on the bottom: 13, 14, 15, 16, 17, 18, 19, and 20. Insert the peg on each leg into the corresponding leg hole.

17 18 19

20

13

14 15 16

## The Great Recyclers

Bugs eat and recycle most of the waste produced by the animals we raise to eat at our dinner tables. This twelve billion tons of waste each year would fill 600,000,000 semitrailer trucks. If lined up end to end, these trucks would stretch to the moon and back fourteen times.

# Bugs Dominate the Earth

In the fall, a spider laid hundreds of eggs on the branch of a tree. A protective silk covering kept the eggs safe through the cold winter. Now it is spring, and hundreds of baby spiders wiggle out of the protective cover. They let out long threads of silk which catch the wind and carry them away to begin life on their own.

Along the ground, a procession of ants carries pieces of vegetables back to its nest. This food will feed the thousands of ants in the colony, which are digging tunnels and caring for eggs containing ants yet to be born.

Nearby, two stag beetles battle each other to determine who will have rights to the rotting log each wants to call home.

Such are the lives of the billions of bugs that inhabit the Earth. Many people try to kill these creeping, crawling, and buzzing creatures, thinking of them as pests that spread disease and devour plants. But bugs are essential for life on Earth to exist. They pollinate crops and other plants. Some eat other bugs harmful to humans or their food plants. Bugs recycle much of the waste from other plants and animals so it can be used to make new plants and animals.

If all humans were to die, the Earth would continue on very well. If all the bugs were to die, the Earth's environment would collapse within a year.

# What's a Bug, What's an Insect, and What's Not

While digging in your backyard, you find a number of creepy, crawly bugs. A six-legged black ant searches for food, while a centipede madly scurries on its many legs to get away from your grasp. A nearby spider dangles at the end of a silken thread, looking for a new home. Most people refer to all these creatures as *bugs*, but none of them is truly a bug, and only one (the ant) is an insect.

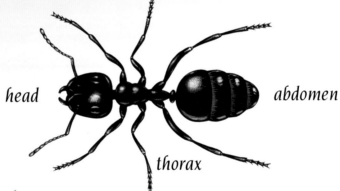

head            abdomen

thorax

All insects have six legs and three body parts: head, thorax, and abdomen, with the legs and wings attached to the thorax. The abdomen holds the heart, digestive system, and reproductive system. Most insects also have wings as well as antennae and two kinds of eyes, simple and compound (compound eyes are made up of many simple eyes).

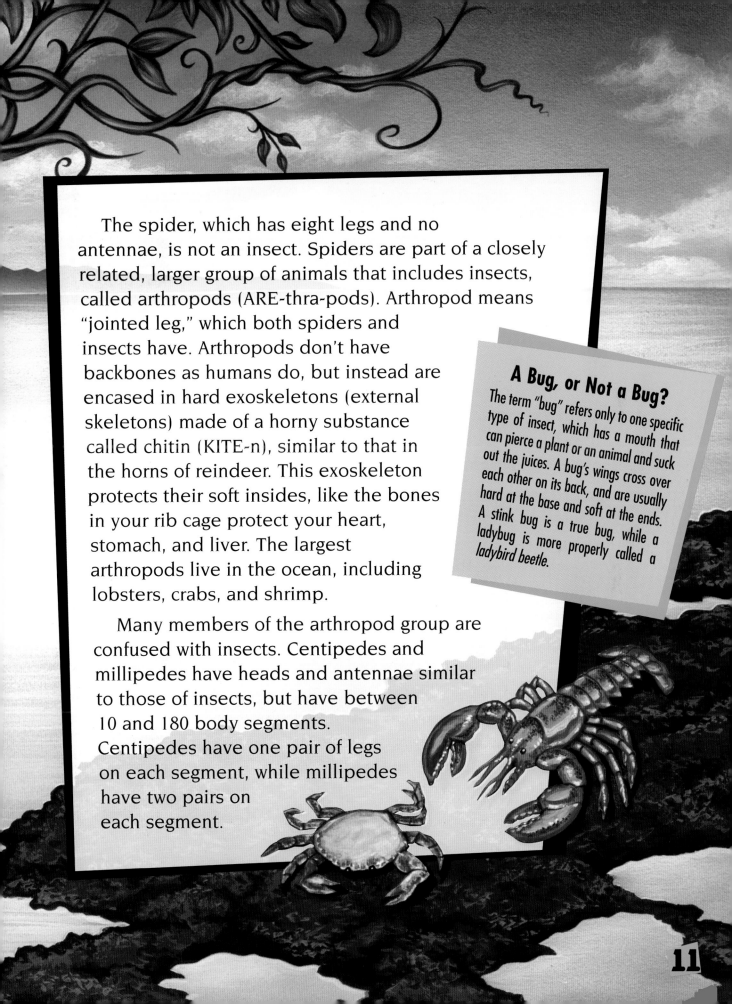

The spider, which has eight legs and no antennae, is not an insect. Spiders are part of a closely related, larger group of animals that includes insects, called arthropods (ARE-thra-pods). Arthropod means "jointed leg," which both spiders and insects have. Arthropods don't have backbones as humans do, but instead are encased in hard exoskeletons (external skeletons) made of a horny substance called chitin (KITE-n), similar to that in the horns of reindeer. This exoskeleton protects their soft insides, like the bones in your rib cage protect your heart, stomach, and liver. The largest arthropods live in the ocean, including lobsters, crabs, and shrimp.

Many members of the arthropod group are confused with insects. Centipedes and millipedes have heads and antennae similar to those of insects, but have between 10 and 180 body segments. Centipedes have one pair of legs on each segment, while millipedes have two pairs on each segment.

## A Bug, or Not a Bug?

The term "bug" refers only to one specific type of insect, which has a mouth that can pierce a plant or an animal and suck out the juices. A bug's wings cross over each other on its back, and are usually hard at the base and soft at the ends. A stink bug is a true bug, while a ladybug is more properly called a ladybird beetle.

# Ladybug

Hundreds of ladybugs crowd into the dark recesses of a little-used corner of a garage, protected from the cold winter weather outside. They huddle together to conserve as much body heat as possible, much as a litter of puppies do right after they are born. The ladybugs are in hibernation for the winter, like many bears and squirrels. By slowing their body functions, they can survive at lower temperatures and do without food or water for several months.

As spring arrives, the ladybugs' body temperatures increase, and they prepare to take flight to find food and water on the vegetation outside. One ladybug opens the hard wing cases on her back, which act like a suit of armor to protect the soft wings underneath. Unfolding her second wings, she beats them and slowly lifts off. She adjusts the tilt of her hard wing covers, which act like the wings of a plane to provide lift and help her change direction. Her destination is a rosebush covered with aphids (A-fids)—small, green insects that eat plants—the only thing she eats.

## Red Means Stop

Because it takes a long time for ladybugs to uncover and unfold their soft second wings, they do not use flight to escape from enemies. A ladybug's "suit of armor" provides some protection, and its bright color tells predators (like birds) that it has a bitter taste.

# A Ladybug Finds Food

Needing food after her long winter nap, the ladybug moves along the stem of a rose covered with aphids. Her antennae, like those on other insects, allow her to smell chemicals given off by other creatures and to sense motion. As the ladybug creeps up the stem, she encounters an aphid devouring the leaf of the rose.

Her two jaws quickly go to work, one directing the aphid into the other. Her jaws move side to side like a pair of scissors to shred the aphid so it can be swallowed.

Weeks later, the ladybug mates with a male ladybug and lays a clump of thirty eggs on the underside of a rose leaf. Her lifelong purpose of laying eggs completed, the ladybug dies. Elsewhere on the plant, a group of eggs laid two weeks earlier are hatching. The baby ladybugs don't look like the adults. They have six legs, but are shaped like little worms and are mainly black with a few orange spots.

## Ladybugs' Spots

Ladybugs aren't just red with black spots! More than 350 different types exist. They come in red, orange, and yellow, and can have no spots or up to fifteen spots. They are one of the most useful insects to humans because they eat aphids, which devour many crops that farmers grow. Thirty ladybugs can protect an entire orange tree, which can produce more than 500 oranges.

# Black Ant

Worker ants scouting for food find a vegetable garden almost the length of a football field away from their nest. Their bodies emit chemical signals telling the other 100,000 worker ants in the nest where to come. The ants pick up the chemical signal with their antennae and follow it to the food.

As the worker ants return to their nest with pieces of vegetables, they descend into a maze of tunnels dug underground by other worker ants. These ants pushed tunnel debris out of the entrance as they dug, which piled up to form a little hill around the tunnel door.

While much of the food is being stored in side tunnels for later use, the most important job is happening deep underground in a remote section of the nest. . . .

## The Herculean Strength of Ants

Ants can carry objects up to fifty times their weight for distances of up to 300 feet. If humans could do this, you could carry a car more than eight miles.

## Ants, Bees, and Wasps

Ants, bees, and wasps have many similar traits. Most species of these insects live in large nests with a single queen that lays all the eggs. The rest of each nest is mainly made up of workers, which find food, clean the nest, and tend the eggs.

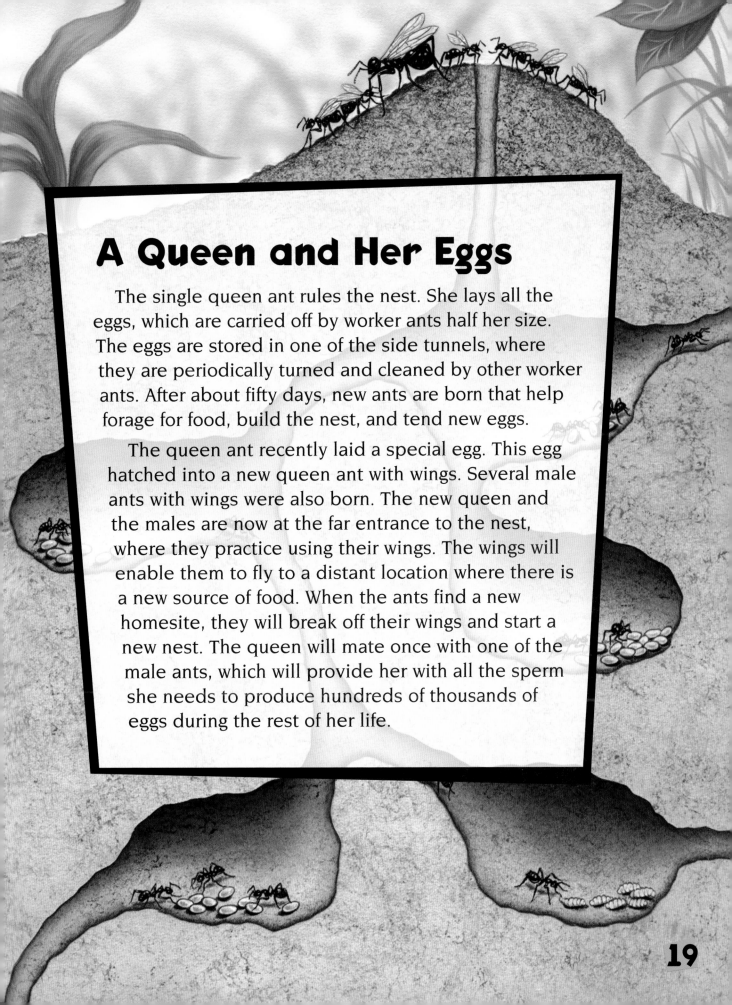

# A Queen and Her Eggs

The single queen ant rules the nest. She lays all the eggs, which are carried off by worker ants half her size. The eggs are stored in one of the side tunnels, where they are periodically turned and cleaned by other worker ants. After about fifty days, new ants are born that help forage for food, build the nest, and tend new eggs.

The queen ant recently laid a special egg. This egg hatched into a new queen ant with wings. Several male ants with wings were also born. The new queen and the males are now at the far entrance to the nest, where they practice using their wings. The wings will enable them to fly to a distant location where there is a new source of food. When the ants find a new homesite, they will break off their wings and start a new nest. The queen will mate once with one of the male ants, which will provide her with all the sperm she needs to produce hundreds of thousands of eggs during the rest of her life.

# Stag Beetle

Two male stag beetles use their enlarged jaws to battle for the right to make a rotting log their home—and the right to mate with the hornless female stag beetle watching the fight from a safe distance. Using his jaws the way deer use their antlers, one beetle rears up on his back legs and twists to the left, trying to flip the other beetle off the log. The two claws at the end of each leg help the second beetle dig into the wood and avoid being toppled. But the leverage of the first beetle is too great. The second beetle loses his grip and lands upside down with a *plop* in a pile of rotting leaves.

The toppled beetle madly waves his legs around, trying to find something to pull against. He finally catches a small twig, to help turn himself over. Having lost the battle, he scurries away to find another place to make his home.

The conquering beetle mates with the female. The log becomes home to them and to future generations of stag beetles.

## The Four Stages of Insects

Most insects go though four stages in their lives: egg, larva, pupa, and adult. Adult insects lay eggs near where larvae will have plenty of food. The egg hatches into a larva, which usually looks nothing like the adult insect. After shedding its skin five or six times over the next few weeks to several years, the larva becomes a pupa, wrapping itself with a protective covering and becoming inactive. The pupa changes into an adult insect and breaks out of its tough covering, ready to find a mate and produce more offspring.

## Beetles Big and Small

There are more than 400,000 kinds of beetle in the world— more than any other kind of animal. The largest is the Goliath beetle from Africa at seven and a half inches long. The smallest is the feather-winged beetle, which is smaller than the period at the end of this sentence.

# A Beetle Egg Matures

After mating, the female beetle begins to lay eggs among the crevices of the rotting log. There is evidence that other stag beetles have laid eggs nearby. A larva burrows into the log using the strong jaws on the front of its head, which is the only part of the larva that resembles an adult stag beetle. Looking more like a worm than it does an insect, the larva uses its sharp jaws to shred the rotting log for food.

In three years the larva will turn into a pupa, after shedding its outer skeleton five or six times as it grows. A nearby pupa is stirring after eight months of changing shape inside its hard covering. It will break out and emerge as a full-grown stag beetle, ready to do battle for a home and mate.

# Greenbottle Fly

Two greenbottle flies hover above a garbage can that is overflowing with the garbage from several meals. After circling each other a number of times, they fly locked together while they mate. The rotting food in the garbage can is the perfect place to lay the 150 eggs growing inside the female fly. Egg clumps from other flies are already visible in the garbage, and several fly larvae—called *maggots*—are getting their fill of food, eating the core of an apple.

The food has been sitting out for weeks and is covered with maggots of many different sizes, each size from a different set of eggs. One maggot is breaking out of its old skeleton—called *molting*—which it has outgrown. Another one has completed its sixth and last molt, and is becoming a dormant pupa. It will stay still for three to ten days while it changes into an adult fly.

## The Many Mouths of Insects

An insect's mouth tells what kind of food it eats! Most insects, like the ant, have jaws designed for chewing. A few insects, including the fly, have mouths with a sponge attached to the end to absorb the juices in rotting vegetation. Other insects, such as the mosquito, have a hollow needle for a mouth, designed to pierce the skin of people and animals in order to suck in blood.

## Survival of the Fittest

Like most insects, flies lay many eggs at a time—up to 250. They can do this every few days for the several weeks that they live. If every baby fly from one adult's eggs survived, a million new flies would exist after one month. But like the eggs of most insects, many fly eggs never hatch. Birds or spiders often eat those that do, or bad weather kills the new flies before they can have too many offspring. Insects lay many eggs to ensure that at least a few will survive.

# A Fly Searches for a Meal

The pesky greenbottle fly got into the house through an open window, and is now seeking a juicy morsel for dinner. The fly's compound eyes provide him with excellent vision. His antennae detect the scent of items good for eating. The pile of sweet corn with butter dripping off it is a good choice. Quickly swooping down on the corn, the fly gently lands and begins sucking up the juices with the spongelike appendage on the end of its mouth.

A person swipes at the fly, trying to kill it. The fly's compound eyes see in many directions at once and the hairs on its body detect any sudden movement, so it escapes without harm. It zooms toward the ceiling, where two drumsticklike structures—modified second wings—allow it to flip over and land with the flight control of a helicopter. Suckerlike pads and claws on the end of each leg let the fly defy gravity to walk around on the ceiling, looking for the next place to swoop down for a juicy meal.

*A fly's head with compound eyes*

# Orb Weaver Spider

Hundreds of newly hatched baby spiders emerge from the protective covering on their egg sack, which an orb weaver spider hid last fall in the notch of a tree branch. Each baby spider lets out a thread of silk for the wind to capture and carry the spider to its new home.

*A spider releases liquid silk*

Another orb weaver spider has already found the perfect home under the eaves of a house. She is squirting liquid silk from the six openings on the end of her abdomen. The silk hardens when exposed to air, allowing her to weave a large circular web with thread so strong it could be made into fishing nets.

When her weaving is done, the spider moves to the center of the web, where she awaits the arrival of dinner. She can't see dinner arrive, since the small eyes on the front of her head can only measure the brightness of surrounding light. But she can feel dinner arrive, using the hairs on her body and legs, which are very sensitive to vibrations. The instant an insect becomes tangled in her web, the spider will spring into action. But for now she sits motionless, waiting for an unsuspecting insect to happen into her web.

## Spiders vs. Insects

Spiders have hard outer skeletons like insects, but they have only two body parts, the head and the abdomen. They have eight legs, no wings, and no antennae. More than 30,000 different kinds of spiders exist, ranging in size from the bird-eating spider, which is bigger than your hand, down to the anapidae, smaller than a pinhead.

## Trap-Door Spiders

Not all spiders weave webs to capture their food. Trap-door spiders dig a hole in the ground and build a small "trap door" at the top to hide under. When an insect passes nearby, the spider springs out of the trap door and captures it.

# A Spider Eats Dinner

A moth flies into the spider's web. The moth wiggles around, frantically trying to escape from the sticky threads. But this only causes him to become more firmly stuck. Feeling the vibrations, the spider charges her captured prey. She injects a poison into the moth using the sharp fangs on the end of her pincerlike jaw. She then wraps the moth in silk for safekeeping until it is time for dinner. When the spider is ready to eat, she uses her jaws to inject digestive juices into the moth, which turn its insides into liquid so they can be sucked into the spider's mouth.

Nearby, a male orb weaver spider carefully approaches the web of a female. If he is not careful, the female will think he is food and eat him before realizing her mistake. The male spider must send the right pattern of vibrations along the female's web as part of his courtship. Only then will he be allowed to approach the female to mate.

Several weeks later, the female spider finds a back corner of the eaves to lay hundreds of eggs surrounded by a protective covering of webbing. Shortly after laying her eggs, the spider dies.

Next spring the eggs will hatch to begin the life cycle again.

# Discovering New Kinds of Bugs

Scientists who study bugs are called entomologists (en-ta-MA-la-gists). They discover hundreds of new kinds of bugs each year, especially in parts of the world where few people live, such as the tropical rain forests of South America. Often a new type of bug looks similar to a bug scientists have already discovered, but with a change that helps the bug survive in a different environment. For example, the hawk moth has an extra-long feeding tube called a proboscis (pro-BOSS-kiss), so it can reach the nectar at the bottom of very long orchids, which provide the moth with all its food.

The rain forest on this page has several new types of bugs. How many can you build using the parts in this kit?